Drug Trafficking

Look for these and other books in the Lucent
Overview series:

Drug Trafficking

by Gail B. Stewart

LUCENT
B·O·O·K·S

LUCENT Overview Series

LUCENT Overview Series

Library of Congress Cataloging-in-Publication Data

Stewart, Gail, 1949–
    Drug trafficking / by Gail B. Stewart.
        p.   cm. — (Overview series)
    Includes bibliographical references and index.
    Summary: Presents a historical overview of drug trafficking
    and discusses its economic and legal aspects.
    ISBN 1-56006-116-2
    1. Drug traffic—Juvenile literature.   2. Drug traffic—United
States—Juvenile literature.   3. Narcotics, Control of—Juvenile
literature.   4. Narcotics, Control of—United States—Juvenile
literature.   I. Title.   II. Series: Lucent overview series.
    [DNLM: 1. Drug traffic.   2. Narcotics, Control of.]
HV5801.S78   1990
363.4'5—dc20
                                                  90-6196
                                                  CIP
                                                  AC

© Copyright 1990 by Lucent Books, Inc.
P.O. Box 289011, San Diego, CA 92198-0011

For my family, Carl, Ted,
Elliot, and Flynn

Contents

1

Introduction

IN JANUARY 1990 Avianca Airlines flight 52 crashed in New York. The plane was taking people from Colombia, in South America, to the United States. Two days later, as surgeons were operating on one of the survivors, they discovered sixteen small rubber containers of cocaine in the patient's intestines. Officials stated that the man, a native of Medellin, Colombia, had been trying to smuggle a pound of cocaine into the United States.

In a run-down housing project on the North Side of Chicago, forty-year-old Shirley Williams has an apartment on the third floor. She has two small sons, and there is a picture on her kitchen wall of a little girl. Williams says the picture is of her daughter, Shala, now dead. Only a few days after the photo was taken, the five-year-old was jumping rope outside, right next to the building, when shooting broke out between warring gangs. Shala was frightened and confused about where to run for cover. She was hit by cross fire and died instantly. Police said later the battle was a dispute between gangs competing for drug-selling territory.

In 1988, a little elementary school in Bogota, Colombia, was bombed. The night watchman had seen a driver slow down and throw something. Seconds later, an explosion leveled the building. Neighbors came running with their jackets thrown on over

(opposite page) Many people think that drugs are only a problem in run-down ghettos, like this one in Chicago. In reality, drug trafficking involves the efforts of thousands of people from all social strata.

Drug agents seized this Colombian cocaine and heroin before it could be transported to the United States. Illegal drugs pour into the United States at staggering rates. Experts estimate that drug trafficking is a $120 billion-per-year business.

pajamas. Children cried because their school was gone. Parents were angry, for they knew why the bombing had occurred. The principal explained that the school—and others like it—had been threatened by the powerful drug organizations operating in Colombia. The organizations were angry because the schools had been teaching students that drugs are bad, said the principal.

Links in a chain

When people think about the drug business, they often think only of secret deals between drug addicts and pushers, or sellers. The drug business, however, is far more complex and involves more than deals between pushers and users. It depends on the efforts of thousands of people who grow raw materials that are made into drugs. The business also depends on people who transport the drugs, chemists who refine them, and people who smuggle them from one country to another. In addition, the illegal drug business needs distributors and wealthy drug "lords" who organize the whole trafficking system.

The cultivation, transportation, refining, and sale of illegal drugs is called *drug trafficking*. Because the trafficking of drugs is illegal, the whole process is cloaked in secrecy. The story of drug trafficking is the story of midnight meetings off the coast of Florida or one of the other millions of hiding places used by smugglers coming into the United States. Because the business must remain secret, people need to be bribed not to alert the police. Often drug dealers bribe border guards and police officers to allow them to continue with their trafficking. One reason such large amounts of money are involved in drug trafficking is because there are so many people participating in the process—so many links in a chain—and all must get their share of the profits.

The profits are immense. In the United States

A smuggler from Colombia sits in handcuffs after a drug bust in Miami. Although the transportation of drugs to the U.S. is dangerous and expensive, the profits are often immense.

alone, drug trafficking is a $120 billion-per-year business. It is a business in which smugglers can spend $500,000 on a speedboat to be used for one night and then abandoned. Traffickers make so much money, in fact, that it is difficult for them to hide it, or even to spend it, without calling attention to themselves.

Although the story of trafficking involves the making of fortunes, it is also the story of poverty. The people who grow the plants from which the drugs are made often live in the most primitive conditions imaginable. These farmers are the first link in the drug trafficking chain. The few extra dollars they make growing these plants often means the difference between starving and being able to afford a little food for their families.

The large amounts of money involved in the drug trafficking business can trigger violence. No one wants to be denied his or her part of the profits, and competition is cutthroat. The drug trafficking story is also one of gang assassinations, murdered police officers, and innocent people caught in the middle. It is the story of bombed schools and newspapers that dare to speak out against the traffickers and judges resigning because they fear for their lives.

Finally, the story of drug trafficking is the story of war. The battles are being waged in locations across the world—from the American cities of New York, Miami, and Chicago to far away places like Bogota, Colombia, and Bangkok, Thailand. And it is not only urban centers that are involved. Tiny vil-

The farmers who cultivate the plants from which drugs are made often live in poverty. Here, Bolivian farmers live in shacks, with no running water or electricity.

lages in China, Burma, and Peru, as well as small American towns are part of the drug trafficking chain. In these places, drug traffickers and those who are dedicated to stopping the massive flow of drugs are engaged in a constant struggle. It is a war that experts agree police and drug enforcement agencies are losing.

To understand the details of this war, it is important to understand how it began. How did illegal drug trafficking become the secret, violent, and profitable business that it is today?

2

The Beginnings of Drug Trafficking

MARIJUANA, COCAINE, and heroin are the three most heavily trafficked drugs in the United States. All three are in demand because they produce positive sensations in many people. All three, however, can produce dangerous side effects, too. Because of the dangers, these drugs are illegal in the United States, as well as in most other nations.

Side effects

Smoking marijuana, for example, usually makes a person feel relaxed and creates a sense of well-being. Users of marijuana say that after smoking the drug, their senses seem sharper. Colors are more vivid; music is more beautiful. But medical experts say there are unpleasant side effects. Marijuana use interferes with memory and the ability to concentrate. Many tasks involving balance and clear headedness—such as driving or following directions—are difficult when a person is high on marijuana.

Like marijuana, cocaine is not usually considered an addictive drug; that is, the user's body does not become dependent on it. However, many users become psychologically dependent on cocaine. That means that even though their bodies are not depen-

(opposite page) A young girl smokes marijuana. Although marijuana is not usually considered an addictive drug, its use is subject to medical and social debate.

15

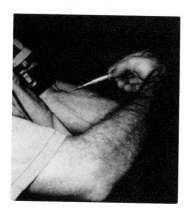

Heroin is often injected directly into the bloodstream, causing what users term a "rush."

dent on the drug, users have strong feelings that they need cocaine to function comfortably. Cocaine users usually feel excited and alert when they are high. They are more talkative and energetic. They feel that they can accomplish anything.

Cocaine can produce dangerous health risks. Cocaine in the bloodstream makes the heart beat faster. It makes the body temperature rise and contracts the blood vessels. In some people, these reactions can cause heart attacks, strokes, or seizures.

Heroin is usually injected by needle into a vein. Heroin users often feel what is called a "rush." This means that there is a quick period in which the user feels very happy and calm. Following the rush, the drug makes people drowsy, and many users go to sleep during this time.

Heroin is an addictive drug. Users feel a physical need to keep taking the drug—usually within several hours of a dose. Without more heroin, users feel anxious or angry. Each time they take more heroin, their bodies require larger and larger doses. This increases the likelihood of an overdose, a dose so strong that it prevents the lungs from functioning. A heroin overdose is usually fatal.

A surprising fact

Because the dangers of drug abuse are so well known, people might think such drugs have been illegal for a very long time. It may surprise them to know that the laws that prohibit the sale and use of drugs like cocaine, heroin, and marijuana were passed less than eighty years ago.

Until that time, these drugs were not only legal in the United States but in some cases were hailed as miracle medicines. For that reason, the trafficking of drugs did not include smuggling or illegal transport. The growing, sale, and use of these drugs was completely open and legal and had been since ancient times.

Cocaine is a good example of a drug that has been used—at least in its base form—for centuries. Cocaine is made from the coca leaf. Archaeologists, people who study ancient civilizations, have unearthed vases containing coca leaves from 2100 B.C.

Coca was an important part of the long-ago Inca empire in Peru. Warriors, nobles, and priests were the chosen few who were allowed to use the drug. It was believed that the coca would give them courage, strength, and wisdom to lead their people. Although the Incas are famous for hoarding great treasures of gold and jewels, coca was as valuable to them as these treasures. Chewing coca leaves gave people energy and strength. It allowed them to do without food or water. It made them forget about the cold or the biting mountain winds.

A magic drug and a thank-you from the Pope

Cocaine was first developed from the coca leaf in Europe in the 1880s. Doctors in the United States were interested in testing it, too. Cocaine was imported in large amounts from laboratories in Europe and in South America, where the coca was grown.

The drug impressed American doctors just as it had impressed Europeans. It was hailed as a magic drug—a cure for everything from nausea and weakness to colds and asthma. Soon there were all sorts of medicines containing large amounts of cocaine. Cough remedies, lozenges, and tonics were popular. One company manufactured a cocaine-filled cigar that could "chase the blues away."

Cocaine was the magic ingredient in a new soft drink called Coca-Cola. It was combined with wine to make a popular drink called Vin Mariani. Vin Mariani was an instant hit with many people, including some celebrities of the day. Inventor Thomas Edison, President William McKinley, and the King and Queen of Norway loved Vin Mariani. Pope Leo XIII even gave the creator of the drink his

A nineteenth-century advertisement touts the benefits of heroin. Drugs that are now considered illegal were used widely in the 1800s. Laws prohibiting their sale and use were not passed until the early 1900s.

official gold medal of honor.

Like cocaine, heroin was thought to be a completely beneficial drug. It, too, comes from a substance that has been used since ancient times. This substance is opium.

Opium—"joy plant"

Opium comes from the poppy flower. The Sumerians, an ancient tribe of people who lived near the Persian Gulf, valued the opium poppy. They called it *hul gil*, which means "joy plant." Sumerians chewed or smoked opium to create a feeling of peace and happiness. In ancient China, too, poor peasants used opium. For them it was a means of escape, a way of temporarily forgetting how difficult their lives were.

When many Chinese immigrants came to the United States in the nineteenth century, they brought opium. It was not illegal for supplies of the drug to be traded or sold in this country. Opium became more familiar to American researchers. In 1806 the drug morphine was developed from opium. Morphine was, and still is today, the most powerful painkiller known.

Heroin is sometimes referred to as morphine's big brother, since it, too, is made from opium. Heroin was invented in 1898 by a chemist who worked for Bayer Laboratories—the same Bayer that today makes aspirin. Some old magazines from the 1890s even have early advertisements for heroin. These ads claimed that heroin was a powerful medicine that would cure even the worst coughs and chest pains. Heroin could be purchased in any drugstore or through the mail. No one knew then how dangerous this drug could be.

Marijuana—"laughter provoker"

Like the substances from which heroin and cocaine are made, marijuana has ancient roots. It is grown in many parts of the world. For that reason, there are records from several places about its use. The Chinese used it as long ago as 2753 B.C. to cure gout, weakness, and absentmindedness.

In India, doctors found that using marijuana made one happy and joyful. A medical book from 1500 B.C. in India called the drug a "laughter provoker." The ancient Egyptians, too, found it useful. They made a special bandage out of marijuana and cloth and applied it to their eyes to soothe them from the hot desert winds.

Marijuana was used by early American colonists but not as a drug. They called it hemp and used its fibrous stems to make strong rope and paper. It was not until the beginning of the twentieth century that marijuana was used as a drug in the United States.

Mexican immigrants knew that the leaves of the plant could be crushed and eaten or smoked. Since ancient times, many tribes of Mexican Indians had used marijuana in religious ceremonies. The use of the drug continued with the farmers who still grew the plant. As more and more Mexicans came to the United States looking for work, the use of marijuana spread. Although marijuana was still considered harmless, scientists in the early 1900s were beginning to suspect the dangers associated with cocaine.

A second look

It may seem strange that such powerful drugs could have been bought and sold so freely in the United States for so long. But during the nineteenth century there were no rules about the testing and sale of drugs, as there are now. The government did not require medicines to be controlled or labeled in any way. There were no laboratory testing procedures that could show whether a remedy might be

A marijuana plant flourishes on a Mexican hillside. The plant's use dates back to 2753 B.C., when the Chinese used it to cure various physical ailments. Ancient Egyptians and Indians also used it for medical purposes.

harmful in certain instances. Harmful side effects were discovered only as more and more people used the drugs.

In the late 1800s, many doctors prescribed heroin for patients. It was known to be a powerful painkiller but did not have the addictive qualities of morphine. After years of use, however, many patients began requiring stronger and stronger doses of heroin to relieve their pain. By the early 1900s many doctors abandoned the drug because it was so strongly addictive.

Like heroin, cocaine was causing medical problems among its users. Sigmund Freud, a pioneer in the science of psychiatry, was a leading advocate of cocaine use in the 1800s. He had taken it himself and had given it to his wife and coworkers. Although Freud called cocaine a "magic drug" at first, he later changed his mind.

Psychiatrist Sigmund Freud was an early advocate of cocaine. He later changed his mind, using scientific data to outline cocaine's negative side effects.

Freud wrote one of the first scientific papers detailing the dangers of cocaine. In the paper he listed several side effects suffered by users. Some people had hallucinations, imagining they saw tiny animals crawling around on their arms and legs. Other people experienced wild shifts in mood, from happy and confident to miserable and confused.

Yet even though many scientists were aware of the dangers, there was a growing number of people who continued to use heroin, cocaine, and other drugs. For these users, the positive sensations they experienced outweighed the possible negative side effects.

Pushing for change

As time went on, more and more people spoke out against the dangers of drugs in the United States. When people could not argue their cases using scientific data, they invented stories about drugs to scare others. For instance, they told stories about men who turned into monsters when they used drugs. These "monsters," they claimed, attacked women and children, and because of their superhuman strength, police officers could do nothing to stop them. Such hysterical stories convinced many people that drugs like cocaine and heroin should be banned from society.

Because popular opinion was against the use of these dangerous drugs, the U.S. government began to take action in the early twentieth century. In 1906, Congress passed the Pure Food and Drug Act. This law made it illegal to sell any food or medicine without stating its ingredients on the label. If cocaine or heroin were contained in a medicine, the amount had to be clearly stated.

Two years later, Congress strengthened the law. Shipping cocaine, heroin, or alcohol from one state to another became illegal. This did not ban the sale of drugs, nor did it prohibit the trafficking of drugs within each state. Each state had its own laws about the use of drugs, and many were banning drug trafficking altogether.

The Harrison Narcotics Act is one of the most famous drug laws in history. It was passed in 1914, and it required that anyone selling, importing, or dispensing drugs had to be registered by the government. From then on, heroin and cocaine could be obtained legally only with a doctor's prescription.

Saying no does not make it so

In 1914 it seemed as if the drug problem were solved, at least from a legal standpoint. No one could abuse drugs if he or she could not get the drugs. And the laws made it clear that drugs could be taken only under strict medical supervision

The United States learned in the coming years, however, that drug use could not be eliminated by passing laws. The growers of opium and coca continued to grow and harvest the plants. Importers continued to bring them into the country. And

somehow, the drugs continued to find their way into the hands of the people who wanted them.

As drug use continued to grow, legislators continued to pass laws. By the mid-1920s, cocaine and heroin were no longer legal, even in medicines. Their sale, use, and transport were strictly against the law. Even marijuana, a much less powerful drug than either cocaine or heroin, was made illegal. By 1937, marijuana was banned in every state.

A law enforcement official smashes illegal barrels of beer during the Prohibition era. Prohibition ended in 1933, when it became apparent that the law was too unpopular and difficult to enforce.

The birth of illegal trafficking

The beginning of drug trafficking as a huge money-making business actually began with the banning of liquor. In 1919 the U.S. government added an amendment to the Constitution. The amendment stated that it was illegal to sell, manufacture, or drink alcoholic beverages of any sort.

The eighteenth amendment ushered in the era of Prohibition.

As with other drugs, however, the law did not eliminate people's desire for alcohol. Some produced their own homemade "brew." Others visited secret after-hours clubs, called speakeasies, that sold illegal whiskey.

Selling and transporting alcohol was illegal, of course, but offered the possibility of making a great deal of money. The demand for alcohol was high, and traffickers could sell as much as they could smuggle.

It soon became clear that individuals working alone could not work as effectively as organizations. It was during Prohibition that many criminals started working together to manufacture, sell, and transport alcohol throughout the United States. The most powerful of these criminal groups was a certain organization of Italian families known as the Mafia.

Prohibition ended in 1933. The amendment banning alcohol was repealed, and trafficking alcohol was no longer illegal. The Mafia could no longer make huge profits because legal suppliers were able to meet the people's demand. Instead, the Mafia turned to the trafficking of illegal drugs—especially heroin and cocaine. Led by Mafia leader "Lucky" Luciano, the crime organization arranged the smuggling and sale of tons of drugs in the United States and other countries around the world.

A booming market for traffickers

The demand for drugs in the United States has not always been constant. Researchers say that the political and social events of a country affect its citizens' drug use. For instance, during World War II drug use by Americans was very low. Drug use at that time was practiced mostly by men, and many men were out of the country fighting the war. It was low, too,

during the time of the Great Depression when people had little money to spend on nonessentials.

Drug use skyrocketed in the 1960s. During that decade, many young people in the United States questioned established ideas of right and wrong. Traditional religious and patriotic values were often abandoned.

Also during the 1960s, drug traffickers became aware that more and more young people were trying drugs. Marijuana was popular because it was fairly cheap. LSD and other hallucinogens were also used in great amounts.

Up until this point in history, cocaine had been considered "the champagne of drugs." It was not as common as other drugs, and because the supply was low, it was more expensive. During the growth of drug use in the United States in the 1960s, however, cocaine became more common. Drug dealers persuaded growers to plant more coca leaves to meet the demand in the American drug market. As the supply of cocaine increased, its price went down. Throughout the 1970s and 1980s, cocaine became the illegal drug of choice for many Americans.

The Drug Enforcement Agency

During the 1980s and 1990s, illegal drugs have flowed into the United States at a staggering rate. The government established the Drug Enforcement Agency (DEA) in 1973 to combat the traffickers, but the agency has not eliminated drug trafficking.

The DEA and other enforcement agencies face enormous problems. They operate on a limited budget, while the criminal organizations that traffic drugs have billions of dollars. The traffickers are heavily armed, and they have an arsenal of high-

A grower stands amidst poppies that will later be used in the manufacture of opium.

tech scanners, radar, and other equipment.

There have been various ideas about how—and where—the problem should be tackled. Some think law enforcement officials should concentrate on the smugglers; others think the pushers who sell the drugs should be caught and punished.

Many people say that the only solution to the drug trafficking problem lies with the drug users. If there were no demand for marijuana, cocaine, heroin, and other illegal drugs, they would certainly not be supplied. On the other hand, as long as people in the United States and other countries are willing to spend billions of dollars every year on illegal drugs, many experts say the problem will not go away. Precisely because the users are so numerous, some argue that law enforcement should concentrate not on the end of the trafficking chain but on the beginning.

The beginning of the drug trafficking chain consists of the growers—the farmers who cultivate the plants from which drugs are made. Advocates of this approach to the problem argue that if there were no opium poppies, coca, or marijuana plants, the drug problem would cease to exist. In other words, the supply of drugs causes the demand for drugs. But there are problems with this strategy. The farmers who now grow these crops have important reasons for continuing to do so. For one thing, farmers and their families use the plants from which drugs are made. For centuries, smoking or eating the plants has offered release from the discomforts of a difficult way of life. In addition, growing such plants pays far more money than growing other crops pays. To a farmer living in a poor village in rural China or in a cave in Colombia, the extra money made from these crops can mean the difference between eating and starving.

3

Why Drugs Are Trafficked

DRUG TRAFFICKING is a huge, multi-billion-dollar business. There are immense profits to be made, especially for those on the end of the trafficking chain. Distributors and dealers inflate the price of the drugs—often by more than 1,000 percent—before the drugs get to the user. A little coca that the grower sold for 80¢ will be refined and processed and sold to a wealthy user for more than $190,000.

The price markup is so high because everyone involved in the illegal drug trafficking chain must get a share of the profits. The trafficking chain is long, and there are huge risks involved. There are hidden factories and laboratories, smugglers and drivers, and millions of people that must be bribed to let the trafficking continue.

The fact that drugs are addictive also keeps the price high. A heroin addict will not refuse to buy heroin because the price seems unreasonably high. He or she needs the drug, and will pay whatever price is demanded. Although cocaine is not physically addictive, as heroin is, it is habit-forming. Cocaine users psychologically need cocaine, so they too pay a high price without complaining.

The people near the end of the trafficking chain

(opposite page) Bolivian police stand in front of a cocaine processing plant in the Bolivian jungle. The camp was raided during a joint Bolivian and U.S. military exercise.

29

become wealthy. They buy sports cars, expensive mansions, and lavish jewelry. They pay bodyguards to protect them twenty-four hours a day. They buy state-of-the-art weapons and equipment that will enable them to bring even more drugs into the United States. One drug lord carried a special gun with a handle made of diamonds and other gems.

There is no limit, it seems, to the wealth of these drug traffickers. But what about the growers? They do not become rich from selling their crops. Why do they continue to farm a product that is dangerous and illegal?

Wealth is relative

Even for the farmers, money is a key reason why they grow marijuana, coca, and opium. Although they do not earn enough money from the sale of these crops to buy sports cars or gold chains, they do make far more than their neighbors who choose not to grow these crops.

One example of this situation occurs in the Chapare Valley in Bolivia. Drug enforcement officials have nicknamed it "Cocaine Alley" because so

In Bolivia, farmers prepare to transport their illegal crop. Although they do not become rich from selling these crops, farmers can triple their income by growing marijuana, coca, and opium.

much coca is grown there. In fact, more than 35 percent of the cocaine that comes to the United States comes from coca grown in the Chapare.

Experts say that nine out of ten people in the Chapare Valley are drug traffickers. Most are farmers who grow coca, but some work in other parts of the trafficking chain, transporting, refining, or smuggling cocaine out of the area. Coca is crucial to the valley's economy. As one researcher states, "Coca is to the Chapare what corn is to Iowa."

Drug traffickers on the other end of the chain are often wealthy. But in the Chapare Valley where the chain begins, there are no rich people. Most of the people there are farmers who are struggling to survive.

Living back in time

One visitor to the Chapare remarked that the people seemed as if they belonged to a different time. They are poor, and they are isolated from other people. They are so isolated, in fact, that DEA squads who go into the Chapare get special hazardous duty pay. The roads and bridges through the mountains are steep and narrow.

The farmers and other traffickers in the Chapare live in homes made of sticks and tin. There are no telephones, no electricity, and no plumbing. The floors of their homes are simply dirt. The only furniture is usually a table. Hammocks serve as beds for a family. People bathe in rivers and wash their clothes the way people did centuries ago—by pounding them on rocks by the riverbanks. The average yearly income in Bolivia is only $565. That makes this country the second poorest nation in the Western hemisphere.

Medical care does not exist in this part of the world, and to reach the age of forty-five is a real accomplishment. Diseases that would be easily managed in the United States are killers in the

In the Chapare Valley, a farmer tends to his coca crop.

mountains of Bolivia. Carol Byrne, a researcher who visited the Chapare in 1989, noticed that people do not rejoice when a baby is born. "They wait until it's old enough to have its first haircut and is relatively safe," she writes. "One of every five babies dies before its first birthday."

Tripling their income

In the Chapare Valley, a farmer can earn three times the average income if he or she grows coca. There is a great demand for it, and the pay is far better than what is offered for other crops.

In 1989, the Bolivian government tried to encourage farmers to stop planting coca. Alternative crops, such as oranges, bananas, coconuts, and pineapples, were suggested. The government even offered to pay farmers five thousand dollars for every acre of coca they agreed to change over to one of these other crops.

But there are still advantages to planting coca. For one thing, coca is an easy crop to grow. It thrives in harsh conditions and does not require special fertilizers or sprays. In addition, coca can be harvested three times a year, unlike the other crops that produce one harvest each year.

Cornelio Soliz Teceros is the mayor of Sinahota, a little town in the Chapare. He sympathizes with the people who want to eliminate cocaine. But the farmers depend on coca, he says, and to prohibit them from growing it would be unfair. "It is our only crop," says Teceros. "When we sell it, that's all we have to live on for three months until the next crop is ready. We get fifty to seventy-five bolivianos [twenty to thirty dollars] per sack for coca, but only one or two bolivianos [forty to eighty cents] per sack for oranges. Why would we grow oranges?"

Similarities in the Golden Triangle

Most of the heroin that comes to the United States is made from opium grown in the Golden Triangle. This is an area where the three Southeast Asian countries of Laos, Burma, and Thailand come together. The farmers here who grow opium are like the farmers in the Chapare Valley. They are very poor, and their lives are extremely difficult.

There are not many crops that can grow on the rocky hillsides of the Golden Triangle. The alternatives for the farmers are fewer than for the Chapare farmers. Wheat will grow there and so will coffee, but the profit to be made from growing opium is three times greater. For a bushel of wheat, a farmer in the Golden Triangle will earn about fifteen dollars; for a little opium, between forty-five and fifty dollars.

Opium, like coca, is also far easier to grow than other crops. And opium poppies fit the style of farming Golden Triangle farmers like best. They wait until the end of the year's rainy season, and then, using large knives and axes, they chop all the trees and bushes out of a large area. After letting the wood dry for a month or so, the farmers burn the area. When the fires have died, the ash that is left is worked into the topsoil. This makes good, rich soil that is just right for the opium poppy.

The farmers are not careful about replacing the minerals to the soil. After a few harvests of poppies, the soil is weak and useless. Nothing more will grow in it, so the farmers and their families simply move to another mountain slope. The process is repeated over and over.

Easier to market

Crops like opium are easier for farmers to market than food crops. The drug traffickers send agents to the farmers to buy their crops. There is no need for the farmers to worry about a treacherous journey to a town market. Because the roads are poor and the travel is very slow, food crops can spoil before a farmer can get them to town.

Opium, on the other hand, stays fresh for about two years, which can also benefit the farmers in another way. If the price traffickers are paying for opium seems too low to farmers, they can keep their crop for a few months. That way, when the price climbs up again the farmers can sell, ensuring a good profit for their work.

A cultural tradition

Some experts claim that even if food crops allowed farmers to make a large profit, farmers would continue to grow opium or coca anyway. That is because both opium and coca are used by the farmers themselves—and by almost all of the people in the opium- and coca-producing countries.

Coca is chewed by the poor mountain dwellers in Bolivia and Peru. "[Coca] has sustained these people for centuries," writes Byrne. "They chew it and

The United Nations has introduced a program for drug abuse control in Thailand. Here, a Buddhist priest speaks to drug abusers at a treatment center in the Buddhist temple of Tham Kra Borg.

A Bolivian mountain dweller smokes opium from a pipe. For many farmers, opium eases the discomforts of a harsh life.

it eases their hunger and their weariness; they brew it into tea and it refreshes them; they take it during childbirth and it dulls their labor pains."

Opium is equally important to the hill dwellers of the Golden Triangle. Opium is smoked, particularly by the old men of the tribe. It is ground into sugar and baked in biscuits and cookies. It is used in religious celebrations and rituals. For many, it has become, as one writer states, what "the cocktail at the end of a day is to people in the West." It helps people relax, and it dulls their pains.

For the opium users, this cultural tradition is accompanied by a long tradition of addiction. Even before opium is refined into morphine and heroin, it is addictive. And the drug traffickers are well aware of the farmers' need for the plant they grow.

Many of the agents who come to the farmers to buy their crop pay them with small amounts of refined heroin. This keeps the farmers, many of whom are addicted to heroin, loyal. The farmers then will continue to grow opium—no matter how much pressure the government puts on them to switch to other crops.

4

The First Links in the Trafficking Chain

ALTHOUGH the equipment and weapons used in the smuggling and distribution of drugs are modern, the same cannot be said for the growing and harvesting of the drugs. Farmers grow and harvest opium, marijuana, and coca in almost exactly the same ways as their ancestors did centuries before.

A legal harvest

Although heroin and cocaine are dangerous drugs, the farmers who grow them do not have to be secretive. In the opium-growing areas of Southeast Asia, and in the coca-producing nations of Peru and Bolivia, these crops are legal. The secrecy does not begin until the next step—the chemical processing and refining that changes coca to cocaine, and opium to morphine and heroin.

A visitor to the Chapare Valley, for instance, would see hundreds of farmers working near the steep slopes of the Andes Mountains. The coca plants grow to a height of six feet before they are ready to be harvested. The farmers walk among the tall plants and strip the leaves from the stalk. They

(opposite page) A farmer in Bolivia displays a leaf from his coca crop.

shove handfuls of leaves into large cloth bags that they wear around their waists. When the leaf gathering is over, the leaves are laid out in a field to dry in the sun.

The process of harvesting the opium is a little more involved but still does not require many tools. The opium in a poppy cannot be removed until the flower blossoms. After the poppy has bloomed and all the petals have fallen off, there remains a pod. The pod is about the size of a golf ball. Inside the

A farmer displays opium pods from his crop in Southeast Asia.

pod is a thick, white, gooey substance that will become opium.

The farmers begin their work in the early evening, when the weather is a little cooler. Using a curved, sharp knife, the farmer makes several cuts in the pod. The sap inside oozes out. As it comes in contact with the air, it turns from white to brown.

The following morning, the farmer returns to the fields and carefully scrapes the brown material from the outside of the pod. This is opium. Each poppy produces a small dab of opium about the size of a pea. The farmer wraps the opium in a petal and puts it in a little box worn around the neck on a rope. As the farmer adds more to the box, the bitter, moldy smell of the substance gets stronger.

An illegal crop

Marijuana is not physically addictive, as heroin is. Nor is it usually associated with dangerous side effects, as cocaine is. Although marijuana is not as dangerous a drug as cocaine or heroin, the growing of it is far more dangerous.

Marijuana can be grown almost anywhere. Much of the marijuana sold in the United States comes from Mexico or Jamaica. Some comes from Colombia. A great deal of marijuana, however, is grown here in the United States, even though it is illegal to grow it.

It is not illegal to grow marijuana in nations such as Jamaica, Mexico, and Colombia, but these countries have tried to cooperate with the United States in eliminating the drug trade. Officials know that most of the marijuana grown in their countries goes north, to the United States. They know that by discouraging farmers from growing marijuana, their countries will have a better relationship with the United States.

Even though growers know the marijuana ends up being sold illegally in the United States, they

When the petals have fallen off of these opium blossoms, farmers will cut the pod with a knife. The substance that emerges will become opium.

A marijuana grower in Mexico tends to his crop. Most of the marijuana in the United States is grown in Mexico or Jamaica.

continue to cultivate the drug. There is a great deal of money to be made from high-quality marijuana.

Marijuana growers have learned to be secretive about their work. In Mexico, marijuana fields are in remote, hilly areas. Farmers create narrow terraces along hillsides. The terraces are flat on top and sharply slanted so that water can drain off. The farmers build in steps along the sharp slopes so that they can easily get to their plants.

The plants require little care, but they do need trimming as they grow. The chemical that makes marijuana a drug is called tetrahydrocannabinol, or THC. In a marijuana plant, most of the THC is found in the top leaves. As the plants grow, farmers pluck off the lower leaves several times a week until the crop is harvested. These leaves are not useful. The plant uses up valuable energy and nutrients making the lower leaves, but the farmers want that energy to be used in creating THC in the upper leaves.

In early fall, after a growing season of six months, the plants grow to a height of eight feet. Plants this tall are ready to be harvested.

Vietcong tactics and window boxes

In the United States, there are many ways of growing marijuana—almost as many methods as there are types of growers. Some marijuana is cultivated in small backyard gardens. One seventy-seven-year-old woman in Oregon found she could earn several thousand dollars each year by selling the eight plants she grew in her window box.

Many of the growers in the United States are farmers. In fact, some government estimates indicate that marijuana is the third most valuable crop for American farmers. In 1985 an estimated $13.9 billion was earned by marijuana crops. American farmers frequently plant marijuana in the same fields as crops such as corn or wheat. That way, it is not so easily detected by police.

In the late 1970s some growers began using government land for their marijuana crops. Many campers and hikers in California's state and national forests were stunned when they were approached by armed men. These men were angry and insisted that the campers leave the forest immediately. In many cases, such men have threatened campers with shotguns or other weapons.

Police officers who were led back to where such incidents happened found large crops of marijuana. The men who threatened the campers were the growers, protecting their crops. In the 1980s and 1990s, the number of these incidents has increased.

Some Americans grow marijuana in their own homes, tending the plant as if it were a houseplant.

Officials list two reasons why growers would choose national forests for their marijuana cultivation. First, there are many thousands of acres of rugged, remote land in the United States. Much of it is inaccessible by road; even an experienced forest ranger could become lost easily. The second reason is that even if the marijuana is found, no one can really be accused of owning it. It would be impossible for police to trace plants on public land to any one person or group.

Besides having armed guards threaten anyone coming near their crops, the growers have created other dangers. Some have set up booby traps, constructed of trip wires. Someone unknowingly stumbling over one of these wires would set off bombs or land mines. Some rangers have reported dangerous traps made of razor blades and knives sticking out of boards. The points of the weapons had been strung at face level in the forest. These traps, known as *pun ji* boards, were used during the Vietnam War by the Vietcong.

Some Americans use public lands to cultivate domestic marijuana. Here, law enforcement officials confiscate a marijuana crop.

Because marijuana growers in these public forests have millions of dollars in drug profits at stake, they are determined not to be driven out. On the contrary, they have been so aggressive that they have intimidated many campers. Growers have shot at cars and have even set fire to ranger stations.

In 1983 the government began a campaign to regain some of the land taken over by these growers. Although they have destroyed many acres of marijuana, officials estimate that there are still over 400,000 acres of park land that are still used by growers—and are still unsafe.

Once marijuana is picked and the leaves dried, there is very little to be done. There are no chemical processes that change the plant. It is used in the same form in which it is harvested—except, of course, that it is crushed and made smaller.

Cocaine in different forms—coca leaves, powder, and crack.

Processing coca

Coca and opium, on the other hand, must undergo several changes before they can be sold as cocaine and heroin to drug users.

After harvesting the coca leaves and drying them in the sun, the farmers sell their product to a representative of the drug traffickers. In Bolivia, for example, this representative might be a member of any one of twenty-eight different drug gangs. It is the responsibility of this drug gang member—usually referred to as a "mule"—to smuggle the coca out of Bolivia and into a Colombian laboratory. There, the coca will be refined into the drug cocaine.

But the coca leaves are very large and bulky. It would be very difficult to transport them in their newly picked form. That is why the growers (or other people in the area) almost always transform the coca leaves into a form that is easier to handle and transport—coca paste.

The coca paste is made in what are called "coca factories." They are not at all, however, what most people think of as factories. Most of the coca factories are hidden deep in the jungles of Peru or Bolivia, far from the eyes of drug enforcement officials. The conversion of coca leaves to paste is the first illegal step in the drug trafficking process.

A factory consists of several pits lined with large plastic garbage bags. Some of the pits are large and deep, others smaller and more shallow.

Each large pit is called a *pozo*. It is in the pozo that the first step of the refinement process takes place. A large amount of coca leaves is put into the pozo, along with sulfuric acid and diesel fuel. These ingredients turn coca leaves into paste. The mixture is allowed to sit in the pozo overnight, or about eight hours.

To speed up the paste-making process, peasants from the village stomp on the leaves and chemicals with their bare feet. The "pozo stomping" goes on all night. Occasionally, the workers take a few minutes to sip some coca tea. That gives them energy to continue their boring task. Each is paid seven dollars for his or her night's work.

The pozo stompers pay a high price for this work in the jungle factories, however. After days and weeks of stomping coca, their feet become diseased and infected. One researcher who visited a factory in the Chapare Valley compared a pozo stomper's feet to dead fish. "The soles are a sickly, pasty, yellowish-white," she writes, "covered with wrinkles, and cracked open." She also noted that the veteran stompers could walk only with hobbling, crippled steps. The infection is permanent.

Making paste

When the stompers are finished with their work, the leaves and chemicals have become an oily, gooey mixture. This substance is moved into small pits, called *fabricas*. In the fabricas the greasy water at the top of the mixture is skimmed off. More chemicals and then a white powder called lime are added. The resulting substance is called coca paste.

The coca paste is not cocaine—it needs to be further refined before it can be used as a drug. That refining is almost always done in laboratories far from the growing areas. The majority of coca paste goes out of Peru and Bolivia, north to laboratories in Colombia.

The coca paste is sold to the "mule" who will smuggle it out of the village. He often wraps the chunks of paste in llama skin. That not only protects the paste from rain and sunshine but also masks the strong smell of the coca paste.

Mules load a private airplane with coca paste. The paste will be transported to Colombia, where it will be refined into cocaine.

A group of peasants wait for the mules who will transport their coca paste to a chemical-processing laboratory.

The grower sells coca leaves for about 30¢ a kilogram. (A kilogram is a little more than 2.2 pounds.) But coca paste is worth far more. For every kilogram—or kilo as it is called for short—the mule will pay between $160 and $200. At each step of the trafficking process, the price jumps.

The mule has more expenses than the grower since he must pay for transporting the paste. There is also far more danger involved in the mule's job. The price he makes reflects those things. Although he has more expenses, he ultimately earns a lot more than the grower or the processor. For every kilo of paste he can deliver to laboratories in Colombia, the mule can earn as much as two thousand dollars.

Transporting the paste

There are a number of ways in which coca paste is transported to Colombia. Sometimes it is taken by car or truck. The risks involved in driving the paste are high, however. Drug enforcement officials patrol the roads through Peru and Bolivia. Suspicious-looking vehicles are often pulled over and searched.

Many mules take advantage of the Amazon River to get their coca paste to Colombia. The river provides a roundabout way of getting from Peru and Bolivia to Colombia. The Amazon twists and turns through some of the most rugged country in the world. It has long been a haven for smugglers—not only of drugs but of weapons, jewels, and rare animal skins.

A more common means of transporting the paste to Colombia is by small private plane. There are hundreds of remote spots where such planes can land. Some of the drug gangs have even built their own private airstrips in the Colombian jungles. Because the airstrips are so hidden, traffickers can often evade police and other drug enforcement officials.

Once in Colombia, the mule takes the paste to

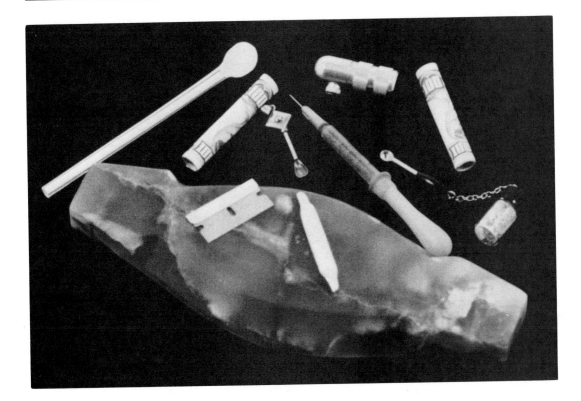

one of a number of laboratories. No one is sure how many of these illegal laboratories are in the country; estimates range from just a few to fifty. Police officers agree that most of the laboratories for processing coca paste are in the large cities. Medellin, Bogota, and Cali have all had laboratories seized by drug enforcement officials.

Some of the paraphernalia employed in the use of cocaine and other illegal drugs.

Making cocaine

The process of changing paste to cocaine is not a long one. There are huge pots into which chemists put fifty pounds of paste at one time. By adding chemicals such as gasoline and ammonia, they can produce a reddish brown substance called cocaine base.

The next step is to add a new batch of chemicals, among them acetone and ether, to the cocaine base. By filtering and heating the mixture, chemists pro-

The processing equipment used to refine cocaine.

duce a fine white powder. This is pure cocaine, ready to be used or smuggled out of the country. Most of the drug will be transported to the United States.

Processing opium

Like coca, opium must be refined and processed by chemists before it is sold as heroin. The refining and processing is often done in laboratories near the growing fields.

The raw opium is transported in a long caravan of horses and mules, accompanied by heavily armed guards. The guards' job is to protect the shipment from police officers as well as from rival opium dealers.

The laboratories, like those used to process coca, are very simple. They are not sterile, gleaming laboratories similar to those found in hospitals and research centers. Because the work is illegal, a heroin laboratory needs to be easy to construct, tear down, and set up in another location, if necessary.

A laboratory in the Golden Triangle region, for instance, is often only a flimsy structure of bamboo. There are a collection of pots and kettles for boiling and some wooden shelves. Drums of chemicals needed to process the opium are lined up around the walls. Drug enforcement officials say that a heroin laboratory can be dismantled in less than twenty minutes.

An example of just how easy laboratories are to set up is seen in the Asian country of Pakistan. Though not in the Golden Triangle area, Pakistan exports a lot of heroin. There were forty-one raids on heroin laboratories there in 1983. Each of the forty-one laboratories was dismantled by the police. Yet officials in Pakistan say that there was no drop in production during that time. Other laboratories had been set up quickly to take over the work.

Morphine, heroin 3 and 4

Before opium can become heroin, it must first be made into morphine, which is an easy process. Opium and water are boiled together, and lime fertilizer is added. The chemist scoops out the frothy

This remote farm in Southeast Asia supplies opium to nearby laboratories so that it can be converted to heroin.

white bubbles at the top of the kettle. After the substance is cleaned and rinsed, ammonia is added, and the mixture is boiled again.

What is left is morphine, a powerful painkiller. Sometimes drug traffickers will decide to process the morphine into heroin at that laboratory. Otherwise, the morphine is packaged into brick-size parcels and shipped to laboratories in Hong Kong or Europe.

If the decision is made to make heroin, the chemists have a more complicated task. The difference between a mediocre chemist and a good one is apparent in this stage of the process. The better the chemist, the more heroin he or she can get from a batch of morphine and the greater the purity of the drug.

To make heroin from morphine requires an industrial chemical called acetic anhydride. This makes

Different forms of heroin seized by the Drug Enforcement Administration.

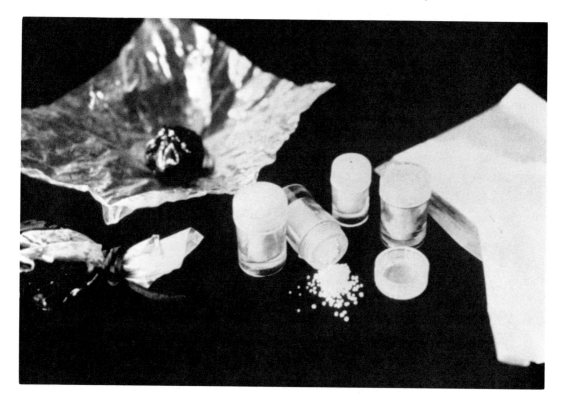

the morphine many times stronger. The two sub-stances are boiled for exactly six hours at a constant temperature. The mixture is treated and purified with more chemicals and then put into a glass bottle called a flask. The final step is the addition of sodium carbonate, which makes heroin crystals fall to the bottom of the flask.

The crystals are whitish brown and are pumped out of the flask. This is called heroin 3. It is the type of heroin that most Asian and European addicts use. It is smoked in a pipe or sprinkled on a cigarette and smoked that way. The kind of heroin American addicts use is called heroin 4. To make heroin 4, the chemist really has to know what he or she is doing, for any mistake could mean a powerful explosion and instant death. Heroin 3 is mixed with more alcohol and other powerful chemicals such as ether. Ether is very explosive, so the chemist must be careful to heat the mixture at exactly the right rate. The pure white crystal flakes that form are heroin 4, the most powerful form of heroin. Drug traffickers call it "China white."

When marijuana is cultivated, and when coca and opium are refined and processed, they are ready to be sold. Although there are some drug users in the countries in which the drugs are grown, the majority of drugs come to the United States. The methods of transporting these drugs to the United States are dangerous and expensive, but they have also been successful.

Opium, morphine, and refined heroin. To make morphine, lime is added to water and opium. Further processing results in heroin that is ready to be sold.

5

Coming to America

SOME OF THE traffickers who move drugs from country to country work independently. They are the exception, however, not the rule. Most of the trafficking—especially in cocaine and heroin—is conducted by large, powerful organizations. These organizations are very efficient. They know the best routes for smuggling drugs. Their members are experts in disguising and hiding drugs passing from border to border. And, because of the unbelievable amounts of money at stake in their trafficking of illegal drugs, these organizations are violent.

The Triads of China

When the opium from the Golden Triangle is processed into heroin, it goes to large cities like Kuala Lumpur in Malaysia, Hong Kong, or Bangkok. Large Mafia-type syndicates, or crime organizations, take control of the heroin. These groups decide where the drugs will go and how they will be transported.

The crime organizations in the Golden Triangle, where most of the world's heroin comes from, are called Triads. The Triads are highly secretive gangs. No one knows exactly how many gangs there are.

(opposite page) San Francisco's Chinatown is one of the largest in the country. Although Triads are centered in China, they operate out of Chinatowns across the United States.

The estimates range from thirty-three to fifty. Worldwide membership in these gangs may be as high as 100,000.

The Triads are centered in China, but they have power in many places. "Any country or city that has a fair-sized Chinese population has Triads," one Drug Enforcement Agency worker claims. "They are the life-support system for the movement of heroin throughout the world. But remember that the Triads don't just control heroin. Throughout Southeast Asia, they control all illegal activity—gambling, prostitution, and the black market for all illegal products."

The Triads in the United States usually operate out of Chinatowns. There are Chinatowns in several cities, but the largest ones are in San Francisco and New York. The Chinese who live in these areas avoid contact with outsiders as much as possible. Most are happier to be left alone to solve their own problems. Police departments in the cities have usually refrained from getting involved with the activi-

Mafia-type organizations often control the flow of heroin in large cities, such as Hong Kong.

ties in Chinatowns. For that reason, criminal organizations such as the Triads have remained hidden.

In Hong Kong, Bangkok, and other cities of Asia, the Triads hire smugglers to take the heroin to the United States and other countries. Once the drugs get to their destination, more Triads are on hand to arrange for the sale and distribution of the drugs. Because they are involved in so many stages of drug trafficking, the bosses of the Triad gangs make billions of dollars each year.

To protect such a lucrative business, Triads are well-armed and extremely violent. If a member breaks the code of silence and gives information about Triad activities to an outsider, he or she is executed. Individuals who interfere with Triad business are killed—whether they are police officers or private citizens.

"Anyone who thinks the Triads can be pushed around or intimidated is kidding himself," says one law enforcement official in Hong Kong. "Killing means nothing to them. We have had instances where Triads want to settle a score with somebody and kill twenty innocent people in the process."

The Colombian cartels

Just as the Triads organize and control the heroin traffic, there are organizations that deal in cocaine. Since most of the coca is processed in laboratories in Colombia, it makes sense that the trafficking organizations are located there.

There is much information in the news about drug cartels in Colombia. The term *cartel* simply refers to a group of influential businesspeople who cooperate with one another. Quite often the reason they work together is to protect themselves from outside competition. They decide how to market their common product and make decisions about the price they want to charge.

The Colombian drug cartels work together, just

Massive shipments of drugs may journey to the United States on large freighters. Officials confiscate only a small percentage of the drugs that illegally enter the country each year.

as legitimate businesses do. They cooperate to protect themselves, however, from police and drug enforcement authorities. They have found that they can be far more successful at trafficking cocaine if they pool their knowledge and connections.

There are several cartels, but the most influential is the one based in the city of Medellin. The leaders of the Medellin cartel are billionaires, and they control many people in Colombia, including some politicians and police. They have connections throughout the United States but have especially strong ties to other Colombians in Miami and New York. When cocaine enters the United States, these people are there to distribute and sell it. In this way, the Colombian cartels are very much like the Triads.

Many paths to the United States

Illegal drugs come into the United States from many directions. Tons of them arrive every year in a variety of ways.

The drug organizations know that unless their product gets safely to the buyer nations, they will not get paid. To make sure the marijuana, heroin, and cocaine get to their destinations, the smugglers know that they cannot do their work in the same way each time. The moment that customs officials or drug enforcement agents can see a pattern in how drugs enter the country, chances increase that the smugglers will be caught. Transporting cocaine on direct flights between Medellin and New York, for instance, would be quite obvious. The goal is to be as unpredictable as possible.

Therefore, the drugs enter the United States in indirect ways. Marijuana from Mexico, for example, may travel to the Philippines by boat, then by plane to Canada, and by automobile to the United States. Cocaine from Colombia may go back and forth to Europe once or twice before arriving in Miami or New York. Heroin from the Golden Triangle may travel to Japan, South America, and Mexico before being carried across the border into Texas.

Such zigzagging is very expensive. One smuggler told a DEA agent that his cartel spent over twenty million dollars just on air and boat transportation each year. Drug organizations know that the profits they make from one shipment will more than pay for the high costs of transporting the drugs.

Illegal drugs are often brought into the United States in small packets containing just a few ounces. But it is the large shipments of several thousand pounds that keep the drug business flourishing in the United States.

Some of the large shipments arrive by small private plane. A smuggler from Colombia flies to Mexico or Panama to refuel and then on to a deserted area in the United States. Usually, such planes fly very low so that they do not appear on radar screens.

A shipment of cocaine is seized. Despite such confiscations, the drug business flourishes.

Boat transportation

A growing number of large shipments arrives by boat. Cocaine, for example, can be sent out of Colombia from two directions. Because Colombia has ports facing both the Pacific Ocean and the Caribbean Sea, the smugglers may choose to ship the cocaine along the west coast of Mexico to a Western U.S. port. Or, they may send the shipments north to the Florida coast.

This type of smuggling involves two boats and sometimes more. The drugs leave Colombia on a large freighter. They are hidden in the storage area, or hold, of the boat. There are hundreds of freighters moving along the coasts of the United States each day, so such a boat draws no special attention.

When the freighter gets fairly close to shore, it stops. If a Coast Guard boat were to get suspicious for some reason and find the drugs aboard the freighter, the smugglers would be arrested. However, if the boat remains at least twelve miles

The illegal cargo of a small, private plane is discovered. The airplane is just one vehicle used to transport drugs into the United States.

off the coast, it is safe. International law says that the oceans outside of the twelve-mile limit are beyond the authority of any one country.

When the freighter gets to its destination off the coast, a second boat makes contact with it. This boat is a powerful speedboat, equipped with ultra-modern scanners, radios, and radar scopes. DEA agents sometimes refer to these boats as "go-fasts," for obvious reasons. The go-fast's job is to carry loads of drugs from the freighter to the shore. A deserted beach is picked out ahead of time, one where no police officers are likely to come by. Some members of the drug organization in the United States watch the site for weeks beforehand, making sure the beach will be safe.

Back and forth the go-fast travels, bringing boxes or crates of the drugs to the designated spot. Often such activity takes place at night, so that Coast Guard boats will be less likely to get suspicious. The go-fasts use no lights, relying instead on electronic sensing devices to help them speed through the dark waters.

A million tricks

But for every large shipment of drugs that comes into the United States, DEA officials estimate that there are five hundred smaller ones. Each day couriers, or mules, from all over the world smuggle in parcels of marijuana, heroin, and cocaine.

Police and customs agents at international airports search baggage and stop suspicious-looking people. But they know that they are fighting a war that they cannot win.

"There are too many bad guys," says a customs agent at Kennedy Airport in New York. "I'm probably not aware of 90 percent of the [drugs] that come through my gate. These guys have a million tricks. I've seen plenty of them. But we can't search everybody—we don't have the staff or the time. Even if we could, these mules can practically make the stuff invisible."

Other law enforcement agents agree. There are thousands of ways drugs can be smuggled into the country unnoticed. Even to a trained eye, the hiding places are sometimes almost impossible to detect.

Drugs have been found hidden in picture frames and sewn into lining of coats. They are packed in-

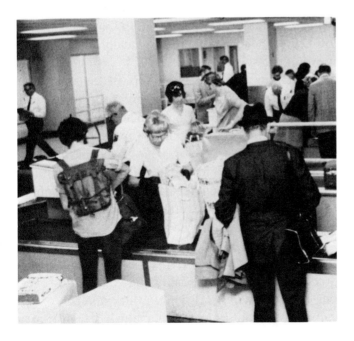

Customs agents at an international airport examine passengers' bags. Because there are so many ways that drugs can be hidden from the view of the agent, most slip by unnoticed.

Drug enforcement agents discover a drug cache embedded in a paddle.

side batteries and within the metal walls of refrigerators. Two million dollars' worth of heroin can be packed inside an aerosol can of deodorant. Marijuana and cocaine have been stuffed into toy dolls and animals and even inside dead bodies in coffins.

Every so often, drug enforcement agents find a new smuggling technique, usually by accident. One such technique discovered in the 1980s is packing drugs inside the layers of a cardboard box, between the perforated edges. The drugs, usually cocaine or heroin, are put into straws and topped off with a few coffee grounds. The coffee helps to mask the scent of the drugs, in case specially trained customs dogs should be sniffing nearby.

Disguising illegal drugs

Another new method of heroin smuggling is to change the form of the drug. Smugglers in the producing country make heroin into a solution by adding certain chemicals to it. Then they soak sheets and towels in the heroin solution. These are sent through customs, almost always with no problem at all. When the sheets and towels are picked up by the contact in the United States, they are chemically treated to retrieve the powdered heroin.

The key danger to a smuggler is, of course, getting caught with drugs. Some smuggling methods, however, can be life-threatening in themselves. One such method is called body-packing. A mule is offered one thousand dollars to swallow bags of cocaine and take an airplane to the United States. The bags, which are called "eggs" by smugglers, are actually small rubber containers filled with several ounces of the drug. The eggs are tied at the top with dental floss.

When the mule arrives at his or her destination, the eggs will be expelled as bodily waste and quickly retrieved. There is a good chance, however, that the eggs will burst while in the stomach of the carrier. The rupture can occur either because of a defect in the rubber or because stomach acid weakens the material. If that were to happen—and it has in dozens of cases—the large amount of pure cocaine in the person's system would cause a massive overdose. The mule would die.

No shortage of help

Even with the dangers of being caught by drug enforcement agents or being killed by body-packing, there are plenty of mules available for work. The drug organizations have no trouble recruiting people.

Drug-sniffing dogs are trained to detect the presence of drugs in large shipments entering the country.

The mules are not actually part of the drug organizations. In many cases, they have no criminal record nor do they understand whom they are working for. The less they know, the less risk they are to the drug cartels or gangs. If they are caught, they will not be able to supply agents with any information about the people who sent them. The organization simply gives a mule the packet of drugs and a set of simple instructions. No names are exchanged, only a phone number to be called upon reaching the United States.

Smuggling methods

Many of the mules are poor people in the drug-producing countries, and they are more than willing to make some easy money. Drug cartels, however, have also recruited college students visiting South America. Tourists returning to the United States from a trip to the Orient are used sometimes. Occasionally, a person is used as a mule without even knowing it.

One such case involved a marijuana dealer from Nevada. He wanted to bring in a large shipment from Mexico but was nervous about being recognized by border officials. Because he made the trip so frequently, he worried that someone might become suspicious.

He put an ad in a local paper, stating that he was willing to rent out his small camper to vacationers. He received several inquiries, but the one he responded to was from two retired schoolteachers. They were eager to travel to Mexico for a few weeks, they told him. To be able to stay in the camper would save them motel money.

While the travelers were in Mexico, a drug dealer there secretly put the drugs in the side panel of the camper. They remained there until the two returned the vehicle to its owner a few weeks later. The travelers were not stopped at the border. They did not look suspicious, nor did they fit the profile of young

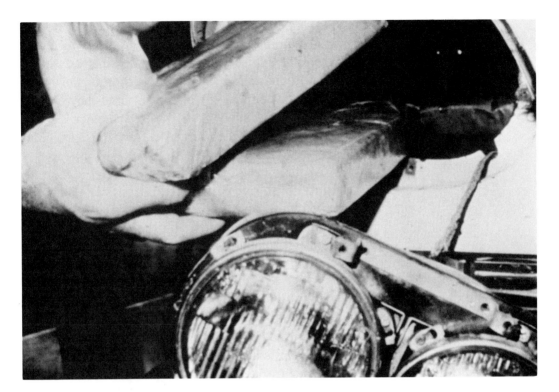

drug users. It was only after the drug dealer was arrested for another crime that many of his smuggling tricks were learned.

Once the drugs have been smuggled into the United States, they begin the stage of trafficking called distribution. Distribution is the process by which the drugs are moved from Miami, New York, and other entry points to cities and towns throughout the country.

A load of drugs is smuggled across the country behind the headlights of a car. Because there are so many hiding places for drugs, stopping their flow is virtually impossible.

Safe houses

There is no one group responsible for the distribution. Instead, there are a series of people who handle the drugs. Often the first step is to take the drugs to a safe house. A safe house is the centralized storage area for incoming drugs. At each safe house people are hired to "baby-sit" the drugs, remaining at the house or apartment twenty-four hours a day.

Drug orders are filled from the safe house. Distributors are hired to drive the drugs to places where they will be sold to other distributors. At this point in the trafficking chain, the drug organizations still have control. The Colombian cartels have people in the United States—often family members—who distribute the cocaine. Chinese Triads or other Asian gangs do the same for heroin.

At this next step, however, the drugs "leave the family," as one DEA official puts it. Both the Colombians and the Chinese have ties with other criminal organizations, and the drugs are sold to them. These people will, in turn, sell to pushers who will then sell to the users.

Distribution in the United States

Until the mid-1980s, Mafia families in the United States were heavily involved with the trafficking of drugs, particularly heroin and cocaine. But their involvement is decreasing, due partly to arrests of key members of Mafia families. In addition, it is far easier today for Chinese and Colombians to keep control over the drugs that are produced in their countries than it is for a Mafia buyer.

From the Chinese and Colombian safe houses, drugs are sold to youth gangs. Some of these gangs are Chinese or Colombian, but many are African-American, white, and Jamaican. These gangs operate in large cities like Miami, New York, Los Angeles, and Chicago. The gangs have names like El Rukn, the Miami Boys, the Crips, and the Bloods.

These gangs existed before the recent increase in the flow of drugs to the United States, but the profits from the drug trade have made them stronger and more violent than ever before. They are armed with assault rifles and specialized automatic weapons. They drive around in Mercedes and BMWs and carry beepers so that they can always be reached when a new drug shipment comes in.

How much profit is there for these gangs? Figures from the DEA in 1989 indicate that some gangs dealing drugs make one million dollars each week. And they spend only about ten thousand dollars on a kilo of cocaine.

Each time the drug changes hands, it is cut, or diluted in strength. Beginning as almost totally pure, it is cut to 70 percent purity by the Colombian distributors and sold to gang members. The gang cuts it again, usually by adding powdered milk, baby laxative, or another tasteless substance. The cocaine is separated into small bags and resold to another distributor, who will cut it again. The $10,000 kilo of cocaine, after being cut and packaged, will bring in over $250,000.   One might think that the police would rather confront gangs of youths than Mafia

Police claim that this gang's main source of income is selling marijuana. The "Ching-a-Lings" are based in New York City's South Bronx.

Crack, a powerful form of cocaine, causes rapid addiction among users.

crime families. Most DEA agents, however, say that they would rather deal with the Mafia. A DEA official from Los Angeles claimed:

> Bring back the mob [the Mafia] any day. These new kids scare the dickens out of me. They have no regard for life or family. There is no code of honor. Everything is money and guns.
>
> The mob were violent, of course, but they had respect for a man's family. A fellow cheated on them, maybe kept some of the drugs himself? They'd kill him, sure. But never his family. These gangs we have now settle scores by shooting a guy's wife and baby.

Gang violence is partly the result of the availability of powerful weapons, according to sociologists. But much of the violence stems from the conditions in which these youths were raised. Most are from ghettos. Their educational opportunities are poor, for most come from families where school is not a priority. They see drugs as an easy way to become rich, they can make more money in an afternoon selling cocaine than they could in a year in a legitimate job.

Violence becomes entwined with the drug trafficking business as rival gangs fight over the right to sell drugs in a certain part of the city. Their battles are fought with automatic weapons. Often innocent people are caught in the cross fire. A drug enforcement official in Detroit explained:

> There has always been crime caused by the presence of drugs in a community. Mostly it was a big rise in burglaries, since junkies [drug addicts] need money to support their habit. But that has really changed in the last five years or so. With the coming of these gangs on the trafficking scene, we have all-out territory wars.
>
> The wars don't just happen in the bad parts of town, either. They are fought in shopping malls or grocery store parking lots, or in the lobby of an apartment building. Millions and millions of dollars are at stake here, and these guys are going to protect it. They couldn't care less who gets hurt.

The distribution of drugs is not limited to the big cities. Users of marijuana, cocaine, and heroin are scattered throughout the United States. The gangs sell their drugs to others who transport them to smaller cities and towns in America.

In many cases, the gangs themselves take the drugs to these other cities. Cocaine and another drug made from it, called crack, have become increasingly popular. Crack is fairly cheap, so it is affordable to many young people. The demand for drugs in these smaller cities has stimulated gangs to expand their activities. The Miami Boys gang, for instance, now has branches in Montgomery, Alabama, and Savannah, Georgia. The L.A. Bloods gang operates out of Kansas City as well. Chicago gangs have spread to Minneapolis, Milwaukee, and even the little town of Racine, Wisconsin.

As these drug trafficking gangs spread throughout the country, they bring not only dangerous drugs but also the violence that seems to go hand in hand with the drug business.

6

What to Do with Dirty Money

DRUG TRAFFICKERS make enormous profits. A CBS report that aired in January 1990 estimated that $120 billion worth of illegal drug business was transacted in one year in the United States.

Every bit of that money is cash, usually twenty and fifty dollar bills. This presents a serious problem for the drug traffickers because such large amounts of cash attract lots of attention. For one thing, huge amounts of bills are bulky and heavy. Drug organizations in the United States do not even take the time to count their money; even with counting machines, the job would take too long. Instead, they use sophisticated microchip scales to weigh the bills. They know, for instance, that 107.4 pounds of twenty dollar bills is exactly one million dollars.

Amounts that large also present another problem. Drug money cannot be reported as income for tax purposes, nor can it easily be deposited in a bank. Federal laws require explanations for large deposits, and drug traffickers cannot afford explanations.

Drug money is known as "dirty" money because it has been made illegally. In order to spend their profits, drug traffickers must "launder" their money. That means, simply, that they must find ways to make the dirty money appear clean, or legal.

(opposite page) Many drug traffickers make so much money that it is difficult for them to hide it without calling attention to themselves.

69

Federal agents display U.S. currency that was seized from an alleged money-laundering operation in New York.

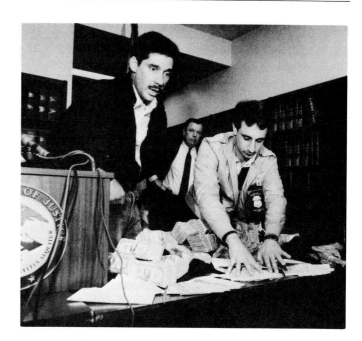

The problem, at least with the U.S. banking system, is that each transaction is recorded. Computers keep track of deposits, withdrawals, and fund transfers. With a "paper trail" to follow, government officials could pursue the traffickers merely by tracking what they do with their money.

Laundering money, say some drug traffickers, is often more difficult than smuggling drugs. However, in recent years, they have found more and more ways to launder dirty money. U.S. banking experts admit that the drug traffickers can usually launder their profits in a forty-eight hour wash cycle. In two days or less, dirty drug money can appear as clean and legitimate as any other earnings in the United States.

Smuggling cash out

Some traffickers prefer to try to get the cash out of the United States. They might take the money back to their own country, such as Colombia, Mexico, or China. Or they might simply take it to a country with banking regulations more lenient than those in the United States.

Taking large sums of U.S. currency out of the country is illegal. Even so, the U.S. Treasury says that it cannot account for the whereabouts of 80 percent of the bills it prints. Drug agents are sure that billions of bills leave the United States each year. Because it is a federal offense, traffickers must be very careful that they do not get caught. Not only would they face penalties for taking money out of the country but they would also have to explain its origins.

The smuggling of money is not as difficult as smuggling drugs into the United States. Customs agents are not nearly as watchful over what people take out as what they bring in. The money is often hidden in trunks, suitcases, and boxes. One Colombian woman was recently caught at Miami International Airport with $1.5 million hidden in a game of Monopoly.

Laundering money

Once the money is safely out of the United States, it is sometimes deposited in foreign banks. Often the money is put into an account set up for a phony company, known as a dummy corporation. There are some countries whose banks thrive on money from dummy corporations. Panama, for instance, has 300,000 such accounts. The tiny Cayman Islands have 14,000. Sometimes, too, the U.S. currency is used to purchase illegal goods on the black market. U.S. money is widely used in black markets all over the world. Most drug traffickers choose not to smuggle the money out of the United States. They prefer to use U.S. banks, both because of the high rate of interest they get on their money and because of the stability of the U.S. banking system. Many countries that readily accept drug money—Panama, for example—do not have a strong economic system. Traffickers do not want to worry that their money will be lost during an overthrow of the government or a military takeover.

By doing business with banks in the United States, however, traffickers face dangers. There is a law that requires the bank to fill out a report for any cash deposit of ten thousand dollars or more. Called a currency transaction report, the form is the government's attempt to discourage drug traffickers from using U.S. banks.

The law in this case has not been completely successful. Banks are often unwilling to turn down deposits because deposits provide the money banks need to survive. For this reason, many have "looked the other way" when large cash deposits have been brought in. As one Miami bank representative stated, "Many of us didn't ask questions because we didn't really want to hear the answers."

Some bankers, however, know exactly where the drug money comes from. They have allowed themselves to be bribed into helping launder it. For a cut of the profits, between 5 and 10 percent, a banker would actively assist a drug trafficker in channeling his money into legitimate operations.

This corruption of banking employees has been widespread, especially in Miami. Because Miami is the entry point for so much cocaine coming into the United States, its banks are flooded with extra cash reserves, most of it in the small bills of the drug dealers. In 1986 it was discovered that Miami banks had more extra cash on hand than all the rest of the U.S. banks put together.

No guarantee

But even if a bank's employees are completely honest and file a currency transaction report on a large cash deposit, there is no guarantee that the drug trafficker will be caught. The U.S. banking industry reports that in 1989 over seven million such reports were filed. The agency that does the investigation of the reports is overworked. It was even difficult for the agency to look into the 100,000 reports each year that was the norm until the mid-1980s. And, since the late 1980s and early 1990s have seen such a drastic increase in reports, agency employees simply cannot follow through on each report.

Laundering smurfs

Drug enforcement agencies say that most drug traffickers do not want to risk making large deposits. Instead, many of them employ full-time help in laundering their dirty money. By making thousands of deposits of under ten thousand dollars, they escape filing the report. As one money laundering researcher noted, however, breaking down millions

Officials hold a news conference behind nearly twenty million dollars seized in a drug raid in New York. Eleven alleged members of the Colombian drug cartel were arrested in connection with this raid.

The profits from drug trafficking are immense. This pile of cash and cocaine was seized in 1989.

of dollars into deposits of nine thousand dollars is as time-consuming as depositing the paycheck of a middle-income person one dollar at a time.

To do the hundreds of weekly deposits, drug traffickers hire "smurfs." Named after the energetic blue cartoon characters, these are people who are paid to stand in line. Hour after hour, every banking day, smurfs make deposits of nine thousand dollars, one at a time, in different accounts, in different banks. For their work, smurfs collect about 2 percent of the money they deposit.

Some smurfs do get caught, however. Even though they are doing nothing illegal (as far as the banks are concerned), they are often recognized. Sometimes bank employees get suspicious and call the police. By following smurfs over an extended time, drug enforcement agents have been able to arrest some of them for laundering money. One smurf, an eighty-two-year-old San Diego woman, had laundered more than thirty-six million dollars in one year. Another smurf was found to have laundered more than five million dollars each week for the Colombian cartels.

Impossible to trace

Once the money is safely deposited in a bank, it can be transferred and moved around from one bank to another, from one country to another. Even without setting foot in a bank, a trafficker can order such transactions by personal computer.

Just as with putting money in a foreign bank, the object is to put the money into something legal, something that can be reported on tax forms without arousing suspicion. Often the traffickers will buy a "front" for the money. A front appears to be a legitimate business, but the drug dealer deposits drug money, rather than legitimate profits, in the business account.

The ideal front for a drug dealer is a business that deals mostly in cash. That way, large cash deposits will seem normal to anyone looking at bank records. Supermarkets, small convenience stores, bowling alleys, and car washes have all been used as fronts for drug traffickers. Once the money is deposited as "car wash profits" or "restaurant profits," it can be withdrawn and spent any way the dealer wants to spend it. And, to the relief of the drug traffickers, the money will be clean.

7

Fighting Back Against Traffickers

ON FEBRUARY 15, 1990, President George Bush traveled to Cartagena, Colombia, to meet with the presidents of Peru, Bolivia, Colombia, and several other countries. The focus of their meeting was the seriousness of the drug problem and drug trafficking in particular.

After the meeting, President Bush proclaimed that the United States would enter into "a new age, a new direction" against the drug trafficking problem. New ideas and increased cooperation among nations would, he stated, help bring the situation under control.

Few people feel optimistic about the chances of stopping the trafficking of illegal drugs. As things now stand, the odds seem to be in the traffickers' favor. Even when one drug dealer is caught and jailed, new ones take his place. Nothing has made much of a dent in the large volume of drugs trafficked worldwide. However, the meeting in Cartagena is evidence that the war against drugs is being taken very seriously. Most people, in Latin America as well as in the United States, agree that the problem has to be addressed promptly.

One Washington politician called the drug problem a "many-headed beast." There are so many

(opposite page) The Drug Enforcement Administration (DEA) was created in 1974 to enforce drug laws. It concentrates on high-level smuggling and distribution in the U.S. and abroad.

This advertisement is part of a campaign to prevent drug abuse.

"heads" on the trafficking chain "monster," it is difficult to know how to destroy it. For instance, should U.S. drug enforcement officials concentrate on the growers or the refiners? Should drug enforcement agents devote all their time and energy to catching smugglers or the gangs that distribute the drugs? And what about the users of illegal drugs? Many people, including Colombian President Virgilio Barco, insist that the drugs would not be grown if it were not for the demand by users in the United States. Some people feel that part of the billions of dollars set aside for the drug war in the United States should be spent on helping users kick their drug habits. Certainly, if no one were interested in buying drugs, they would not be trafficked. The United States, more than any nation on earth, seems to have an insatiable appetite for drugs. Many people believe that until drug demand is decreased, there is no hope of stopping the heavy flow of drugs into the United States.

Fighting drug trafficking

Another opinion, however, is gaining acceptance with many experts. They believe that the way to win the war is to sidestep it entirely. They say that by legalizing the drugs that are now illegal, the country could rid itself of the crime and violence caused by the illegal distribution and sale. The price of the drugs would come down because there would be no long trafficking chain handling the drug shipments. The lower price would mean that addicts could afford the drugs without committing crimes to get money for their habit. Money now spent on fighting drug trafficking could be spent helping addicts. The drug problem, say legalization supporters, would become a medical problem, not a political or law enforcement problem.

There have been many proposals suggested recently on how to stop the flow of drugs into the

U.S. drug czar William Bennett wants to increase the budget for drug law enforcement.

United States. Some of the proposals require the cooperation of the drug-producing nations; others could be implemented by the United States alone. All of the new ideas require a great deal of money.

In the past, it was believed that a campaign to educate people about the dangers of drug abuse would help. Former First Lady Nancy Reagan, for example, started her "Just Say No to Drugs" campaign with this technique in mind. The idea was to take a message to the young people of America that even though drugs and drug traffickers are powerful, young people are powerful, too. They could "say no" to pushers or other people who urged them to use drugs. By decreasing the demand, the traffickers would have to decrease the supply.

Former First Lady Nancy Reagan speaks to a group of students as part of her "Just Say No" campaign.

That method has not worked, according to U.S. drug policy director William Bennett. The number of drug users in the United States is estimated at 14.5 million, and many medical experts call it an epidemic. What is more frightening, say such experts, is the climbing rate of people addicted to heroin and crack cocaine.

Bennett has stated that he favors stiffer penalties for drug users. He wants a bigger budget for law enforcement and demands the prison system be enlarged to accommodate all of the people who break the drug laws.

He also believes, as do other drug enforcement experts, that the real war on drug traffickers cannot take place in the United States, or even at the borders. The thousands of miles of unguarded border between Mexico and the United States, for instance, cannot be patrolled every hour, every day. There are not enough customs workers, DEA agents, or police officers to seal off the borders from drug smugglers.

Edward Lopez, a DEA agent working in southern Texas, agrees that fighting a war against traffickers at the borders is futile. "I could run along the border every day—just a mile or so—and I wouldn't catch a tiny fraction of what comes in. We don't have the manpower, and [the drug traffickers] know it."

Many officials involved in the drug war agree. They feel that the best way to stop drugs is to get closer to the source. "We can run along the border forever and try to catch loads as they come," says Charles Gutensohn, DEA's head of cocaine investigations. "Or we can go down to [Peru and Bolivia] and try to stop the flow out."

Waging the war on foreign soil

Some of the new plans are aimed at the source of the drugs. For instance, President Bush wants to place radar stations in the mountains of Peru, Bolivia, and Colombia. The radars would locate small planes being used to transport drugs. Whenever a plane could be tracked, the radar station would alert the aircraft carrier *John F. Kennedy,* which is always stationed off the coast of Colombia, on the Caribbean side. Planes from the *Kennedy* would immediately be sent up to intercept the drug smugglers, forcing them to land before they could transport any drugs.

Another well-publicized strategy to combat cocaine trafficking goes even closer to the source. It is aimed at the growers of coca leaves in Peru and Bolivia. In February 1990 Bennett announced that the United States was spending $6.5 million on developing ways to destroy the coca plants while they are growing. One of the most interesting ways is to release millions of malumbia caterpillars into the fields and let them feast on the coca. These caterpillars would quickly destroy the harvest.

There have been plans to give billions of dollars

Drug enforcement officials raid a field of coca-growing crops. William Bennett feels that the plants should be destroyed before they make their way into the American marketplace in the form of illegal drugs.

in aid to drug-producing nations, also. Concentrating his efforts on the cocaine traffickers, President Bush wants to supply Colombia and other affected nations with guns, helicopters, tanks—anything it takes to help those countries fight the traffickers within their borders. In addition, Bush has pledged economic aid to coca-growing nations. Much of the money will be used to encourage farmers to grow crops other than coca.

The United States has met with some resentment, however, on the part of several Latin American countries. They were angered by the U.S. invasion

DEA agents prepare to enter a building suspected of housing a chemical processing plant.

of Panama in December 1989 and the arrest of Panamanian dictator Manuel Noriega on drug trafficking charges. Although few Latin American leaders liked Noriega, and no one denies his role as an aid to drug traffickers, they feel the United States overstepped its boundaries. Many foreign policy experts agree that the United States must assure its friends in Latin America that it will not take such an aggressive role in their countries.

"Beyond the needle in the haystack"

Although many ideas and strategies have been proposed for fighting drug trafficking, many people think that winning the war on drugs will be a difficult task. They say that there are many obstacles, many factors working on the side of the traffickers.

For instance, one often-heard proposal for fighting drug traffickers urges the government to increase its use of DEA agents for conducting searches in foreign nations. The idea would be to intercept the transport of drugs before they came to the United States. DEA agents insist that they already do conduct searches in other countries. They collect information and are sometimes even given tips on what types of vehicles are transporting the drugs. Together with the police of that country, DEA agents set up roadblocks and search the vehicles. In spite of their best efforts, however, most of the drugs are never found.

The DEA forces in Thailand are a good example. They know that most of the heroin coming out of the Golden Triangle travels on two main roads in Thailand. But there are many vehicles that travel those roads. Some are ten-wheel trucks, some are vans and pickups, others are government cars. The agents know that the drugs could easily be hidden in any one of those vehicles.

The drugs could be hidden among thousands of

This affidavit for a search warrant resulted in the seizure of powdered cocaine and crack.

Deposed Panamanian leader Manuel Noriega is accused of aiding the laundering of drug money.

sacks of rice on their way to market. The drugs may be hidden in fish frozen in ice blocks or even in cow manure to be sold as fertilizer. As one DEA agent remarks:

> It would take five men and an entire day to carefully go through one ten-wheeler. And the whole time you're tying up traffic. Remember that this is only a two-lane road, and when you pull a ten-wheeler onto the soft shoulder it ties up traffic for miles. And there are hundreds of trucks like that each month.

The hiding places are endless. As one U.S. official states, "It's beyond a needle in a haystack. First you need to figure out which haystack to look at." There is also a limit to the inconvenience a foreign country will put up with to help the United States in its fight against drug traffickers. If agents come up empty-handed in a search, the foreign police will be less willing to aid them the next time.

Buying accomplices

A troubling aspect of the war against drug traffickers is the bribery and corruption it causes. The people who allow the traffickers to continue their illegal business without worry of being caught are everywhere in the trafficking chain. From top government officials down to police officers on the beat, the drug traffickers have ways of getting the help of other people.

Sometimes people are bribed with large sums of money. Manuel Noriega is said to have received millions of dollars for aiding in the laundering of drug money. He also has been accused of being paid for helping cocaine factories secure the large amounts of chemicals needed to process the coca.

The prime minister of the Bahamas, too, came under fire in 1989 for letting his country be used by drug traffickers. According to leaders of the Medellin Cartel, Prime Minister Lynden Pindling accepted hundreds of thousands of dollars in exchange for letting drug traffickers land in the Bahamas to refuel. Private planes do not have fuel tanks large enough to make a trip from Colombia to the United States. They need to stop and refuel. According to some drug traffickers, they even jokingly referred to the Bahamas as "our aircraft carrier."

Heroin traffickers, too, have corrupted many government workers. For instance, the Eastern European nation of Bulgaria has been called "a smuggler's paradise." Traffickers transporting large amounts of heroin into Europe from Iran or Turkey must pass through Bulgaria. KINTEX, the Bulgarian customs agency, is routinely alerted by smugglers when a shipment of heroin is about to pass through. KINTEX is given a description of the vehicle and its li-

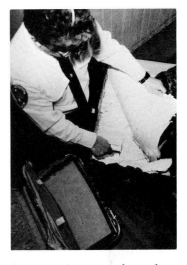

A customs inspector shows the false bottoms of suitcases used by heroin smugglers.

cense number. When the vehicle comes to the checkpoint, it is waved through.

In Hong Kong, Triad gang members have close contacts with workers in the government shipping offices. The workers are paid to change invoices on crates traveling to the United States. Invoices list the country from which a crate was originally mailed. However, crates from Thailand or Burma would surely be searched, for they are key heroin-producing nations. The shipping workers change this information. They list more innocent-sounding countries on the invoice, such as South Korea, which is not part of the drug trafficking chain.

Corruption and police

Police officers, too, are frequently paid by drug traffickers. Many are offered large sums of money—or quantities of the drugs themselves—in exchange for favors. Such bribes are sometimes difficult to resist. One Chicago police officer, a veteran of twenty years, was offered a bribe larger than all the money he had made in his whole career. Unfortunately, the instances of bribery and corruption are many. In his book *The Cocaine Wars,* researcher Paul Eddy estimates that one out of every ten Miami police officers has been "bought" by drug money.

Corruption within their own departments tends to make law enforcement officers feel cynical and hopeless. They wonder if the work they do is worth the effort. Such thoughts could result in lazy police work, say some experts. Confidence is lost, replaced by doubt and distrust of fellow officers.

Corrupting police and government officials has been relatively easy for drug traffickers. In the South American cocaine industry, the traffickers give officials a choice—"*plomo o plata,*" or "the silver or the lead." In other words, officials can choose to take the silver (the money) as a bribe, or they can take the lead (as in bullets). They are either

A young woman injects heroin. Drug addiction is one of the many factors sustaining the drug trafficking business.

paid or, if they refuse to be bribed, killed.

Threats such as these have resulted in many corrupt officials. The threats have also resulted in an unbelievable number of murders. In the town of Medellin alone, one thousand public officials were murdered by drug gangs in the last ten years. Police chiefs, judges, supreme court justices, and cabinet ministers: anyone who dared to fight the cartel was simply executed.

People in Colombia and other drug-producing nations continue to fight the cartels, although the violence has frightened many into silence. Judges in Colombia are resigning by the hundreds, choosing to quit rather than have to try a drug case.

No signs of letting down

There is another aspect of the war against drugs that worries many people. Despite efforts to show the danger of drugs, drug use in the United States has increased. New drugs with strange names like "Hawaiian ice" and "crank" are being trafficked

Forensic chemicals used to determine the purity of illegal drugs.

into the United States. Experts say that these are more powerful and addictive than cocaine or heroin.

There have been changes, too, in the more established drugs such as heroin and marijuana. According to DEA agents, the heroin that is being sold on the streets today is far more dangerous than the heroin of five or ten years ago. The danger comes from the strength of the drug.

In 1988, however, DEA agents found that the heroin being sold on the streets of New York and other large cities is 40 percent pure. The reasons for this drastic rise in strength are not completely understood, although some have guessed that it is a result of the drug changing hands less often. Since the Triads keep control of the shipments both in Asia and in the United States, the heroin may not be cut as often as before. Whatever the reason, the heroin on the streets today is far more addictive. Users are now much more likely to die of an overdose of the drug.

As its purity has increased, some of heroin's other risks have decreased, making it seem more safe to addicts. Of the two types of heroin manufactured by chemists in the Golden Triangle—numbers 3 and 4—heroin 4 has long been the type of heroin sold in the United States. It is injected into the body with a needle. Needle sharing by addicts, however, has been pointed out as a common way the AIDS virus spreads. As a result, 3, which is smoked, is becoming more common. Addicts do not have to worry about needles. Drug enforcement agents worry that the decreased threat of AIDS will make heroin 3 more appealing to young drug users.

A brand new industry

Some of the most drastic changes in the trafficking of drugs have occurred with the marijuana growers. Scientists have found new ways to breed a variety of marijuana that is much stronger than the drug that was sold two or three years ago. The THC content, the active ingredient in marijuana, has always been in the range of 3 to 5 percent. The new strain of marijuana is far more potent, with THC levels of 16 or 18 percent.

New farming techniques have helped marijuana producers grow more of this new powerful marijuana. Much of it is being harvested indoors. Growers use high-intensity lamps, conveyor belts, timers, fans, sprinklers, and automatic fertilizing machines. DEA agents say that such marijuana "factories" can turn out three crops every year, whereas outdoor growers can only harvest one crop.

Government officials and others worried about the drug problem are especially concerned about these improved growing methods and the more powerful drugs being used today. They are concerned, too, about the slim chances of apprehending smugglers, the corruption of public officials, and the violence associated with drug trafficking. All of these things are obstacles to winning the war against drugs.

Yet although many experts disagree on the odds of stopping the trafficking of drugs, no one has suggested giving up. Many have urged, however, that the United States change the focus of the drug war.

"My hope is that somehow we can come to terms with the fact that we can never stop the criminals from bringing the stuff in," says drug treatment worker Terry O'Gara. "There is too much money in it for them to fold up shop and go home. But maybe we can do something to eliminate some of the reasons people buy cocaine, crack, heroin, and other drugs. Self-respect, jobs, lots of things can turn an addict into a person with a real life again. Maybe we could try that—after all, nothing else has worked."

Glossary

addictive: The property of a drug that makes a person physically crave it.

body-packing: Swallowing small containers of drugs to smuggle them past customs officials.

cartel: An organization of business people that makes decisions about the price and marketing of a product.

coca: The large tree-like plant from which cocaine is made.

coca paste: The product of the first step in refining coca. Coca paste is made by combining coca leaves with lime, sulfuric acid, and other chemicals.

crack: A drug made from refined cocaine. Crack is cheap, plentiful, and highly addictive.

cutting a drug: Diluting, or weakening, the substance by adding powdered milk or baking powder to it.

distribution: The transport of drugs from the point of entry to cities and towns across a wider area.

drug trafficking: The cultivation, sale, and distribution of illegal drugs.

dummy corporation: A phony company, set up as a bank account to launder drug money.

go-fast: A high-tech speedboat used by smugglers to unload a large drug-carrying ship offshore.

heroin 3: The form of the drug that is smoked.

heroin 4: The form of the drug, common in the United States, that is injected into a vein.

kilogram: A unit of weight, equal to approximately 2.2 pounds.

laundering: The process of changing the cash received from drug deals into untraceable, "clean" money that can be banked and declared on tax returns.

morphine: A painkiller made from opium.

mule: One who carries illegal drugs from one country into another.

opium: The sap inside a poppy from which morphine and heroin are made.

safe house: A centralized location where illegal drugs are stored.

smurfs: People hired by drug traffickers to stand in bank lines to launder money.

THC (tetrahydrocannabinol): The chemical contained in marijuana that makes that plant a drug.

Triad: A secret, violent gang organization with origins in China. Triads are responsible for the trafficking of much of the heroin that comes to the United States.

Suggestions for Further Reading

David Browne, *Crack and Cocaine*. New York: Gloucester Press, 1987.

Paul Eddy, *The Cocaine Wars*. New York: W.W. Martin, 1988.

Nigel Hawkes, *The Heroin Trail*. New York: Gloucester Press, 1986.

Thomas Hoobler and Dorothy Hoobler, *Drugs and Crime*. New York: Chelsea House, 1988.

Eva Stwertka and Albert Stwertka, *Marijuana*. New York: Franklin Watts, 1979.

James Traub, *The Billion Dollar Connection*. New York: Julian Messner, 1982.

U.S. News & World Report, "A Slaughter of Innocents," July 10, 1989.

Steven Wisotsky, *Breaking the Impasse in the War on Drugs*. New York: Greenwood Press, 1986.

Geraldine Woods and Harold Woods, *Cocaine*. New York: Franklin Watts, 1985.

Works Consulted

Carol Byrne, "Cocaine Alley," *Star Tribune Newspaper of the Twin Cities,* November 6, 1989.

Rick Dolphin, "A Global Struggle," *Maclean's*, April 3, 1989.

James A. Inciardi, *The War on Drugs*. Palo Alto, CA: Mayfield Publishing Co., 1986.

Douglas Jehl and Robin Wright, "Cracking the Cartels," *Star Tribune of the Twin Cities*, September 3, 1989.

Maclean's, "Battling Crime Through the Banks," May 29, 1989.

R. Moran, "Bring Back the Mafia," *Newsweek,* August 7, 1989.

Gerald Posner, *The War Lords of Crime*. New York: McGraw-Hill, 1988.

Tina Rosenberg, "The Kingdom of Cocaine," *The New Republic,* November 27, 1989.

Eloise Salholz, "Hitting the Drug Lords," *Newsweek*, September 4, 1989.

Time, "Attacking the Source," August 28, 1989.

Index

About the Author

Gail B. Stewart received her undergraduate degree from Gustavus Adolphus College in St. Peter, Minnesota. She did her graduate work in English, linguistics, and curriculum study at the College of St. Thomas and the University of Minnesota. Gail taught English and reading for more than ten years.

She has written forty-eight books for young people, including a six-part series called *Living Spaces*.

Gail and her husband live in Minneapolis with their three sons, two dogs, and a cat. She enjoys reading (especially children's books) and playing tennis.

Picture Credits